NUMBER 453

THE ENGLISH
EXPERIENCE

ITS RECORD IN EARLY PRINTED BOOKS
PUBLISHED IN FACSIMILE

The publishers acknowledge their gratitude to
the Syndics of Cambridge University Library
for their permission to reproduce the
Library's copy, Shelfmark: Syn.8.53.48

Library of Congress Catalog Card Number:
72-6027

S.T.C.No. 21587

Collation: A-F^8

Published in 1972 by

Theatrvm Orbis Terrarvm Ltd.,
O.Z.Voorburgwal 85, Amsterdam

&

Da Capo Press Inc.
-a subsidiary of Plenum Publishing Corporation-
277 West 17th Street, New York N.Y. 10011

Printed in the Netherlands

ISBN 90 221 0453 2

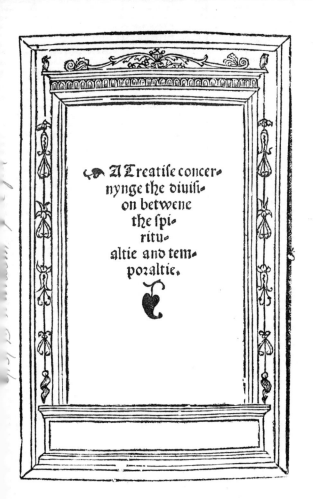

❧ A Treatife concer-
nynge the diuifi-
on betwene
the fpi-
ritu-
altie and tem-
poꝛaltie.

¶

This lyttell booke declareth dyuers causes, wherby diuision hath rysen betwene the spiritualtie and temporaltie: and partly sheweth, howe they may be brought to a vnite. And if they that may do moost good towarde the sayd vnite, wyll take the articles of this treatise, as lyttell tytlynges to bryng som weyhtier thynges to theyr mynde concernyng the same, and thanne by theyr wysedomes wyll adde them herevnto, and (as they shall thynke necessarye) to see them all put in due execution: J thynke veryly, that in shorte tyme they shall brynge this matter to good effecte, to the honoure of god, τ to the comon welth and quietnes of all the kynges subiectes.

℧Dyuers articles, whiche haue bene a
speciall cause of the diuision that
is betwyrt the spiritualtie
and the temporaltie
in this realme.
The fyrst Chapiter.

 Vho maye remembre the
state of this realme nowe
in these dayes, without
great heuynes and sorow
of herte? For there as in
tymes paste hath reygned charite/meke
nes, concorde, and peace, reygneth nowe
enuye/pryde/diuision/and stryfe: and
that not onely betwene laye menne and
laye men/but also betwene religious
and religyous/and betwene preestes
and relygyous/and that is yet more
to be lamented, also betwene preestes
and preestes. Which diuision hath bene
so vniuersall/that it hath ben a great vn
quietnes and a great breache of chariti.
through all the realme: and parte of ie
hath rysen by reason of a great singulat
rite, that religious persons and preestes
haue hadde to theyr estate of lyuynge/

A.ij.   wherby

wherby many of them haue thoughte
theyr eſtate moſt perfite befoꝛe all other.
And ſome of them haue therby exalted
them ſelfe in theyr owne ſyght ſo hygh/
that they haue ryſen in to ſuche a ghoſtly
pꝛyde/that they haue in maner diſday-
ned and diſpyſed other, that haue not
lyued in ſuche perfection as they thynke
they doo. And of this hathe folowed,
that ſome of them haue hadde vnſyt-
tynge woꝛdes of the other/callyng them
flatterers, diſſimulers, and hypocrites:
And they haue called the other ageyne
pꝛoude perſons, couetous/vayne gloꝛi-
ous/and louers of woꝛldely delytes/
and ſuche other.

⸿ And an other parte of this dyuyſion
hath ryſen by dyuerſities of opynyons,
that haue ben vpon the auctoꝛities, po-
wers, and iuriſdiction of ſpirituall men
amonge them ſelfe. And vpon theſe dy-
uyſions ſome laye men haue in tyme paſt
fauored the one parte/and ſome the o-
ther: wherby the people haue greatly
be inquyeted. But J wote not fully by
what occaſion it is, that nowe of late
the great multytude of all the laye people

ple haue founde defaulte, as well at prestes as relygious, so ferfourthe that hit
is nowe in maner noted through all the
realme/ that there is a great dyuysion
bytwene the spiritualtie and the temporaltie. And veryly it is greatte pytie that
suche a noyse shulde sprynge and go a-
brode. And some alledge dyuers causes
why hit is so noysed. Fyrste they saye,
that neyther preestes nor religious kepe
not the perfection of theyr ordre to the
honour of god and good example of the
people/ as they shuld do : but that some
of them procure theyr owne honour, and
call it the honour of god/ and rather couet to haue rule ouer the people than to
profyte the people. And that some couet
their bodily ease and worldely welthe,
in meate and drynke and suche other ,
more than commenly any temporal man
dothe. And that some serue God for a
worldly laude, and to be magnified ther
fore/ more than for the pure loue of god.
And somme laye men saye farther, that
though religious men haue varied with
religious, and that some prestes haue va
ryed also with religious in some pointes

concernynge the preemynence of theyr
perfection, as is sayde before: that yet in
suche thynges as perteyne to the mayntenaunce of the worldlye honour of the
churche and of spirituallemen, whiche
they call the honour of god, and in such
thynges as perteyn to the encrece of the
riches of spiritual men, religious or secu
ler, they saye they agree all in one. And
therfore they say, that all spiritual men,
as to the multitude / be more diligent to
enduce the people to suche thynges / as
shall brynge ryches to the churche, as to
gyue money to trentals / and to founde
chaunteryes and obytes, and to obteyne
pardons, and to go vpon pylgremages,
and suche other : than they be to enduce
them to the payment of theyr dettes, to
make restitutions for suche wronges as
they haue done / or to do the werkes of
mercye to theyr neyghbours , that be
poore and nedy / and that sometyme be
also in ryght extreme necessite.

℃ And for as moche as it is most commenly sene / that amonge a great multitude there be many, that worke rather
vpon wyll than vpon reason, And that
                              though

though they haue a good zele, yet many
tymes they lacke good ordre and discretion, whiche is the mother of al vertue.
Therfore some persons thynkynge that
worldely honoure and ryches lettethe
greatly deuocion, so moche that as they
thynke, they can nat stande to gyther,
haue holden opinion, that it is not laufull to the churche to haue any possessions. And some takynge a more meane
waye therin, haue sayde/that as they
thynke, it is laufull and also expedient,
that the churche haue possessions: but
they thynke, that the greatte haboun-
dance, that is in the churche/doth great
hurt, τ induceth in many of them, a loue
to worldely thynges, and letteth and
in maner strangleth the loue of god.
And therfore they thynke, that it were
good to take awaye that is to moche/
and to leue that is sufficient. And some
also, as of a policie to pull ryches fro
the churche, haue inveyed ayenste all
suche thynges as brynge ryches to the
churche. And bicause great riches haue
comme to the churche for prayenge for
soules in purgatorye, haue by wordes
affirmed

affirmed / that there is no purgatozie:
And that grauntynge of pardons riseth
of couetyse of the churche, and pzofy-
teth not the people/ and that pylgremages be of no effecte, and that the churche may make no lawes, and such other
thynges / as foundynge of chaunteries,
making of bzotherhedes/ and many mo.
Wherin they shewe outwardly to ryse
ageynst all the thynges befoze rehersed,
and to dispyse them/ and yet they know
and beleue in theyz hartes/ that al these
thynges be of them selfe right good and
pzofytable / as they be in dede / if they
were ozdered as they shulde be. And
somme persones there be/ that thzoughe
grace fynde defaute onely at the abusion
and mysse ozder of suche thynges, and
speke nothynge ayenst the thynges selfe,
neyther of purgatozie/ pylgremages, settynge vppe of ymages / oz suche other.
Foz they knowe well, they be ozdeyned
of god, and that the mysozder rysethe
onely of man foz couetyse, singularite, oz
some other suche lyke defaulte/ thzough
perswasion and disceyte of the goostely
ennemye. And thoughe some men haue
                                    mysta-

myſtaken them ſelfe in the ſayd articles,
yet dyuers other haue ſayd, that if they
had ben well and charitably handeled/
they myghte haue benne reſourmed,
and paraduenture ſaued in bodye and
in ſoule.

⸿And vpon al theſe matters there is ry
ſen a great opinion in the people, in maner vniuerſally, that in punyſſhyng and
correccyons all theſe perſons beſore reherſed ſhulde haue lyke punyſſhement/
if ſpirituall men myght haue free lyber-
tye in that behalfe. And that ſpiritualle
men wolde, if they coulde: as well put
them to ſilence, that ſpeake ayenſt the a-
buſion or diſordre of ſuche thynges, as
be beſore reherſed, as them that ſpeke a-
yenſt the thynge ſelfe. And many other
murmours Ꝝ grudges beſide theſe that
be beſore reherſed/ be amonge the peo-
ple/ mo than J can reherſe nowe: but yet
aboue all other me thynketh that hit is
moſt to be lamented and ſorowed/ that
ſpiritualle men, knowynge theſe grudges and murmuracions amonge the peo
ple/ and knowynge alſo that many layc
men haue opinion, that a great occaſion

therof ryseth by spirituall men, and that
they do no moze to appease them, ne to
ozdre them selfe in no other maner foz
the appeasynge of them , than they do.
Foz al that they do therin most cōmen-
ly is this : they take hit , that they that
fynde defaute at suche abusions and dis-
ozdre, loue no prestes : and therfoze they
esteme, that they do of malyce all that
they do, to distroy the churche / and to
haue theyz goodes and possessions them
selfe : And therfoze they thynk it a good
dede to se them punysshed, so that they
shall not be able to bzynge theyz malyce
to effect. And therfoze haue they punysshed many persons / which moch people
haue iuged them to do vpon wyl, and of
no loue vnto the people. And though spi
ritual men are boūde in this case, foz ap-
pesing of these opinios in the peple / whiche be so daūgerous as well to spirituall
men, as to tempozal men, that many sou
les stonde in great peryl therby, not onely to refozme them selfe, and to leue and
auoyde all thynges , that gyue occasion
to the people, so to offende, that may by
charyte be omytted and lefte / but also to

fast, pray, weare the heare, gyue almes,
and to do other good dedes for them
selfe and for the people, cryenge conty-
nually to our lorde, that these diuisions
may ceasse/ and that peace and concorde
may come agayne into the worlde: yet
it appereth not that they do so, but that
they rather contynue stylle after the olde
course / pretendynge by confederacies
and worldly polycies, and streyte cor-
rections, to rule the people/ and that is
greatly to be lamented, and it wyll be
harde for them to brynge it so about.
But if they wolde a lytell meken them
selfe, and withdrawe suche thynges as
haue brought the people into this mur-
moure and grudge: they shulde anone
brynge a newe lyght of grace in to the
worlde, and brynge the people to per-
fecte loue and obedience to theyr supe-
ryours. And here me thynketh I might
saye farther in one thynge / and that is
this, that as longe as spiritualle rulers
wyll eyther pretende, that theyr auctoritie is so hygh, and so immediatly deri-
ued of god/ that the people are bounde
to obeye them/ and to accepte all that
they

they do and teache, without argumentes resistence or grudgynge ayenst them, or that they wyll pretende, that no defaulte is in them, but in the people, and wyll yet contynue styll in the same maner, and after the same worldly countenance, as they do nowe, and haue done late tyme paste: The lyght of grace that is spoken of before, wyll not appere, but that bothe parties shall walke in this darkenes of malyce and diuision, as they haue done in tyme paste.

⁋An other occasyon of this diuision. The seconde Chapyter.

THere haue bene made in tyme past many good lawes by the churche for the good ordre of spirituall menne, whiche were right necessarye to be kept to this day: whiche nowe be altered eyther by a lawe made to the contrarye, or by somme euylle custome brought vp and suffered ageynste them. And I shal brefly recite some of them, as
I haue

J haue founde them wꝛytten by other
befoꝛe this tyme.

℃ Fyꝛste there was a lawe made, that
a man well appꝛoued in his werkes and
doctrine ſhulde be made a byſſhop/and
not a chylde ne a carnall man, oꝛ that is
vnlerned in ſpiritual thinges.

℃ Alſo that nothynge ſhulde be gyuen
in any place foꝛ burialles, confeſſion, gyuynge of oꝛdres, ne foꝛ any of the ſacra-
mentes, noꝛ foꝛ any pꝛomocion.

℃ Alſo that byſſhops and pꝛeſtes ſhulde
not be atte vayne woꝛldely ſyghtes oꝛ
pleys, ne delyte in them.

℃ That it is not laufull foꝛ a byſſhoppe
oꝛ pꝛeeſte to be abſente on the ſondaye,
but to be at Maſſes/and that faſtynge.

℃ That no pꝛeeſt ſhulde eate fleſſhe from
Quinquageſime to Eeſter.

℃ That pꝛeſtes ſhuld faſte aduent.

℃ That byſſhoppes and pꝛeeſtes / and
eſpecially monkes and religyous, ſhall
ſtudye in heuenly ſcriptures, all lernyn-
ges and pꝛactiſes of litigious thynges
lefte aud ſette aparte.

℃ That the byſſhop ſhall euery yere go
aboute his dioces with great diligence,
and

and effecte.

¶ That heuenly scriptures be redde at the byſſhops table.

¶ That a clerke fulle of fowle woꝛdes ſhall be put fro his offyce.

¶ That the wages of clerkes ſhalbe gyuen after theyꝛ merites.

¶ That preſtes ſhall eſchewe feaſtes at mariages.

¶ That clerkes ſhall comme in no tauernes.

¶ That a byſſhop ſhall haue pooꝛe apparell, lodgyng/ and table / and fedynge foꝛ pooꝛe men.

¶ That a byſſhop ſhal not lightly ſtriue foꝛ tranſytoꝛie thynges.

¶ That clerkes ſhuld rather ſtudie, that theyꝛ bꝛetherne that varye, be bꝛought to peace, than to iudgement.

¶ That a clerke ſhulde inſtructe euery man with his woꝛdes, and to the entent that pooꝛe men ſhuld not be greued/that they ſhulde get theyꝛ lyuynge with ſome handy crafte, as ſaynt Paule dyd.

¶ That clerkes ſhall not take vppon them the actes oꝛ pꝛocuracyons of ſeculer men.

That

❡That laye men ſhall not make clerkes
theyr factoures or gouernoures vnder
them.

❡That monkes after the counſeylle of
Calcidonence, ſhalbe holly entendynge
to faſtynges and prayers in the places
where they renounced the worlde, and
that they forſake not theyr monaſteryes
for no buſynes of the churche ne of the
worlde.

❡That clerkes that cuſtomably be play
ers at tables or hunters, ſhalbe prohybit
of houſlynge. And ſaynt John Chryſo-
ſtom vpon Mathewe the. xxi. Chapiter
ſayth/that as of the temple cometh out
all goodnes/ſo of the temple al euyll pro
cedeth. And therfore it foloweth, that
if preſthode be hole, all the churche flo-
riſſheth: And if it be corrupte/the fayth
and vertue of the people fadeth alſo and
falleth awaye: as if thou ſe a tree that
hath wethered leues/thou knoweſt ther
by that there is a defaut in the rote/ſo
whan thou ſeeſt the people lyue out of
good ordre, knowe it for certayne, that
theyr preſthode is not hole ne ſounde.
And therfore if it were aſked/where is
nowe

nowe the deuocion and obedience of the inferiours/the defence of knyghtes, the peace of Christen pryncis, to the ende that they beynge at a concorde, myghte resiste and seyght agaynst sismatikes and infydels / recouerynge ageyne regions, whiche they haue nowe taken fro christen men, and peruerted them: It myght be answered/that they be gone through brekynge of suche lawes.

¶ Many of these sayenges and dyuers other here omytted, be the sayenges of John Gerß chancseller of Paris, in a tretice that is called in latin Declaratio defectuum virorum ecclesiasticorum. In whiche treatise he recyteth also dyuers abusyons, wherof I shall recyte parte vnder the maner of questions for shortenes, as he doth / as wel cöcernyng other countreyes as this, that they maye the rather be knowen and auoyded.

¶ Fyrst he asketh this question. What it auaileth/or what profiteth the church the superfluous pompe of prelates and cardinalles, and what meaneth it?

¶ Also that one man hath. iiii. v. vi. or viii. benefyces, wherof he is not percase worthy

worthy to haue one, wherwith.viii.per
sons might be susteyned, that gyue them
selfe to lernyng/prayer/ꝛ to the seruice of
god? Here(saythe he)take hede. Whether hors, dogges, byrdes, and the superfluous company of men of the churche shulde rather eate the patrimonie of
the churche / than the poore menne of
Christe/or that it be expended in the seruice of god, and to the conuersion of in-
fidels / or in suche other werkes of mercye and pietie? O howe many places
(saythe he) ordeyned for the seruice of
god in Rome and elles where / be nowe
through the negligence of prelates deso
late ꝛ distroyed? O how is it sayth he,
that the swerde of holye churche, that
is the sentence of Excommunication,
to her owne dispite and reproofe, is so
lyghtly drawen out: and for so lyttell a
thynge (as sometyme for dette)is so
cruelly executed vpon poore men? What
is it also, that one cause vppon a smalle
thynge shall contynue so many yeres?
and why is not that lengthe of tyme,
whiche is the spoyler and robber of
poore men, in somme conuenient maner

cutte away? why is it not rather mer-
cifully appoynted to the Jewes conuerted, somme reasonable lyuynge of theyr
owne goodes rather than by extreme ne
cessite to compelle them to forsake the
faythe ageyne, and to reproue chrysten
men / that they be cruelle and haue no
pitie? Judge ye also (sayth he) whether
so great varietie of ymages and pictures
be expedient: and whether they do not
peruert som simple persons to ydolatrie?
But here hit is to be nooted / that Johñ
Berson fyndeth not defaulte in settynge
vp of ymages, for he commendeth it in
many places of his werkes, but he fyndeth defaute at the varietie of them in
theyr peyntynge and garnysshyng with
golde / syluer / precious stones, and suche
other / with so great riches about them,
that some symple persons myght lyghtly be enduced to beleue some special wor
kynge to be in the ymages, that is not in
them in dede. And so he fyndeth defaute
at the abuse of ymages: and not at the
settynge vppe of ymages. Discusse also
(sayth the sayd Johñ Berson) whether
so large exempcions as somme haue, be
expe-

expedient꜕ and whether it be profytable
so to leade them froo theyr ordinaries？
Serche also saythe he , if there be not
some apocrisate wrytynges, or prayers,
or hymnes by processe of tyme (somme
of purpose, some by negligence) brought
vp to the hurte of the faythe？ but than
he asketh : whether all prelates and prestes be gyltie in the articles aboue rehersed, and he saythe our lorde forbede it.
For lyke as Helyas , whan he had went
that all the people of Israell hadde bene
fallen to ydolatrie , herde our lorde say／
I haue yet reserued seuen thousand mé,
that neuer bowed theyr knees before
Baale : ryghte so it may be sayde , that
nowe in these dayes our lorde hath reserued ryghte many good menne bothe
spiritualle and temporalle ／ that be not
gyltie in any of the sayde articles ／ ne
yet partie in any maner to the sayd diuisyon , whiche throughe helpe of grace ,
and with the fauoure of the superiours
shall be ryghte well able to brynge the
other to good accorde.

¶ An other occasyon of this
dyuysion.
The thyrde Chapiter.

Here be many lawes and decrees made bi the church wherin it is recited, ꝗ laici sūt clericis infesti, that is to saye, that laye men be cruel to clerkes/and therfore the church hath therypon made dyuers lawes to opresse that crueltie/as in them appereth. And therypon hath folowed, that whan prestes haue red the lawes, they haue iuged therby/ that theyr reulers haue knowen some great crueltye in laye men agaynst clerkes. For elles they wolde not haue put tho wordes in to theyr lawes/ and that hath caused many spyrytuall men to adiudge the more lyghtly, that suche thynges as laye men haue done concernynge them/hath rather ben done of malice and cruelti than otherwise/and that iudgement in processe of tyme hath caused them to confedre them selfe togyder, to resiste that malice/ whiche they many rymes by occasion of the sayde wordes,
haue

haue iudged to be greatter than it was/
and haue many tymes recyted the wor=
des, affermynge them to be true : and
therfore they haue extended all lawes,
that be made agaynst laye men the more
extremely ageynste them : wherby the
people in many countreyes haue bene so
ofte greued and oppressed, that they
haue grutched maruayllously at it. And
whan lay men haue redde tho wordes,
they haue také therby, that the makers
of tho lawes, whiche represent in them
the estate of all spirituall men/haue iud=
ged that the makers therof thoughte/
that laye men were cruell agaynst them :
and where crueltie is iudged to be,there
is no loue. For lyke as nothyng helpeth
more to noryslhe loue in a man/than that
he maye knowe/ that the other louethe
hym/ though he neuer receyued any pro
fyte by hym : so nothynge noryslhethe
more diuision and discorde/ than that a
má know that an other loueth him not,
though percase he know, that he neuer
dyd hym hurte, ne entendeth not to do.
And therfore whan lay men haue by tho
wordes taken occasyon to thynke, that

spyrytuall men haue adiuged crueltie in
them: they haue anon iuged, that spy=
ritual men loue them not, and that hath
in their hartes broke the charitable loue
and obedyence, that they ought to haue
to spyrytuall reulers: and thoughe the
occasion of this artycle be not vniuersall
(for all laye men haue not sene tho wor=
des) yet the reporte of tho wordes hath
come to the knowlege of many lay men,
as well by spyrytuall men as by temporall men, that haue redde them: which
by longe contynuance hath noryshed
one great branche of this diuisyon / whiche I suppose veryly wylle neuer fullye
be appeysed, tyll the spyrytuall gouer-
nours wyl be as dilygét to make lawes,
that shal brynge in mekencs amonge spy
rytuall men, and that may enduce them
charytablye to suffre some tyme them
that offende them / as they haue bene in
tyme past to make lawes to set spyrytuall men in suche case / that they may cor-
recte all them and kepe them vnder, that
wyll any thynge resyste them. And lyke
as many spirituall men haue mysordred
them selfe ageynste laye men, not onely
in

in ſuche thynges as be partely touched
before / but alſo in wordes, affermynge
ſomtyme, that laye men loue not preſtes:
ſo in likewiſe ſome lay men miſordre thē
ſelfe in wordes agaynſt preſtes, and wyll
ſaye / that there is no good preſte / or that
all preſtes be nought : and ſome, as it is
ſayde / wyll call them ſomtyme horeſon
preſtes . And if all theſe wordes were
prohybyte on bothe ſydes vpon greate
paynes / J thynke it wold do great good
in this behalſe.

An other cauſe of this
dyuyſion.

The fourthe Chapyter.

Þe harde τ extreme lawes
that are made for layenge
vyolent handes vpon cler-
kes , and ſuche other ſpyrytuall perſones, hath ben
an other cauſe of this diuiſion . For they
be verye parciall / as to the reders wyll
appere , and they be alſo ſo generall /
B 4   that

that nether kynge noz lozde be not excepted in them, but that they shulde goo to
the pope to be assoyled . And the sayde
lawes be . xvij . q . iiij . si quis suadente
diabolo et eẍ. de sentenc.excõmunicac.ca.
Non dubium, et ca. mulieres/ et La. per-
uenit: et ca. ea noscitur. ⁊ in many other
chapiters there, et eẍ. de sentenc. excom-
municac. li. vi. ca. religioso . And these
lawes be suche, that if a manne in violence lay his hande onely vpon a clerke/
that he is accoursed : but thoughe a
clerke bete a laye manne wzongefully,
and with violence, he is not accoursed .
And this parcialyte hath done greatte
hurte .

CCAn other occasyon of
this diuision.
The fyfte Chapyter.

Doughe there be dyuers
good and reasonable arty-
cles ozdeined bi the church
to be redde openlye to the
people at certayn dayes by
the churche therto assygned/ which com
menly

menly is called the generall sentence : yet
many curates and theyz paryſſhe pzeſtes
ſometyme rede onely parte of the artycles, and omytte parte therof, eyther foz
ſhoztnes of tyme, oz els to take ſuche artycles as ſerue mooſte to theyz purpoſe.
And ſomtyme, as it is ſayd, they adde o-
ther excómunications after their mynde,
that be not putte in to the ſayde generall
ſentence. And whan the artycles be ſo
choſen out, they ſounde to ſo great parcialite and fauour foz ſpirituall men, eyther foz payement of tythes, offerynges/
moztuaries, and ſuche other duetyes to
the churche, oz foz the mayntenaunce of
that they calle the lyberties of the churche, as that no pzeeſte noz clerke ſhall
not be put to anſwere befoze laye men,
ſpecyally where theyz bodyes ſhulde be
arreſted/ oz that no impoſitions ſhulde
be layde vpon the churche by tempozall
power, oz ageynſte them that with violence lay handes vpon pzeeſt oz clerke, oz
ſuche other : that the people be greatly
offended therby/ and thynke great parcialite in them/ and iudge them rather to
be made of a pzyde and couetyſe of the
churche :

churche: than of any charite to the people, wherby many doo rather dispyse them than obeye them. And J suppose veryly, that this diuisyon wyll neuer be perfytely and chariably refourmed and broughte to good accorde, tyll the people come to this poynt / that they shall greatly feare and drede to ronne in to the leeste censure of the churche. And that wyll neuer be, tyll the heedes spyrytuall wyll refourme them selfe, and shewe a fatherlye loue vnto the people, and not extende the sentences of the churche vppon so lyghte causes / and vppon suche parcialyte, as they haue doone in tyme paste. And if they wyll refourme these poyntes before rehersed / and somme other hereafter folowynge, J suppose veryly the people wylle gladdely here them and folowe them. For than, as the gospelle saythe / they be theyr verye shepardes. Wherfore if it were ordeyned as well by auctoritie of parlyamente as of conuocation, that suche artycles shulde be deuysed and putte in to the generall sentence, that shulde styrre as well spyrytuall

tuall menne / as tempozalle menne to
loue vertue / and flee vyces / to loue
trouth and plainnes/and to flee falshode
and doublenes, and that none vppon a
payne shulde adde oz dyminysshe any
thynge concernynge the sayde articles:
J thynke it wolde helpe moche to make
a good agrement of this diuision, and to
contynue the same / with loue and drede
betwixte the reulers spirytuall and the
people / as there oughte to be. And if
lyke articles were deuised to refrayne
spirytualle men fro gyuynge hereafter
any ferther occasion to this diuision, oz
any other lyke: and they to be redde at
visitations/Scenes, and suche other like
places/where preftes asséble by cōmande
ment of theyz ozdinaries, with certayne
paynes to be appoynted by parlement ꝼ
conuocacion: J thynke it wolde bzynge
many thynges in to good ozder / and
helpe moche to a good refozmation of
this diuision.

⸿An other occasion of this
diuision,
The sixte Chapiter.

An

An other occasyon of this diuision hath partely rysen bi temporal men, that haue desired moche to haue the familyaritie of preestes in theyr games and disportes, and haue vsed to make moche more of them that were compenable, thanne of them that were not so/ and haue called them good felowes and good companyons. And many also wolde haue chapleyns, whiche they wolde not onely suffre/ but also commande to go on huntynge/hauking, and suche other vayne disportes. And some wolde let them lye amonge other laye seruauntes, where they coulde neyther vse prayer nor contemplation.

℩ And some of them wolde suffre them to go in lyueries / not conuenyent in colour for a preste to weare; and wold also many tymes set them to worldely offices, as to be bayliffes, receyuours, or stewardes: and than whan they haue by suche occasion bene moche beaten, and greatly exercysed in suche worldely busynes / so that the inwarde deuocyon of the harte hath ben in them as colde and

as

as weke in maner / as in laye men / yet if
any benefyce haue fallen voyde of theyr
gyft, they wolde preferre them to it, eyther as in recompens of theyr busynes
and labours, or for that they were good
companions : rather than another good
deuoute man / that percase is lerned, and
kepeth hym selfe fro suche wordely va-
nyties and ydle company / or that is dis-
posed somtyme to admonysshe charyta-
bly suche as he is in company with / of
suche defautes as he seeth or hereth of
them / and that fewe mē do loue to here:
And therfore wyll they preferre them /
that wyl let them a lone. And yet whan
they haue so done / they wyl anone spcke
euyll of prestes, and reporte great lyghtnes iu them, and lyghtly noote one preste
with an nother prestes defaute / and that
whan they haue bene partly occasioners
to theyr offences them selfe / as it is sayd
before. And this demenor hath through
a longe contynnaunce norysshed some
parte of this dyuysion / and so wyll it do
as longe as it cōtinueth. And also where
by the lawe, prestes oughte to be at the
churche on sondays and holy dayes, and
helpe

helpfoorth the seruice of god in the quere,
and ought also whan they be there, to
be ordered by the curate: yet neuer the
lesse many men that haue chappeleynes,
wyll not suffre them to come in the parysshe churche, and whan they be there,
they wyll nat haue them ordered by the
curate but after them selfe: ne see them
be in the quere, but sendeth them many
tymes on other errandes, and that in
woorldly matters, as customably as they
doo other seruauntes: and many suche
chapleynes shewe them selfe euidentely
by theyr diligence in that behalfe, to be
better contente to do that busynes, than
to be in the quere, and that maketh the
curates and the neyghbours bothe to
thynke a great lyghtnes in them, and do
discomende them for it, and whan they
here of it, they be also discontented, and
theyr may feers bothe, and say the paris-
shes haue nothynge to do with it, and
commenly other chapleyns wylle take
parte in suche matters: wherupon dyuers grudges and variances haue rysen
in many places, that haue done greatte
hurt in this behalfe. And as it is in this
case

case of chapleyns, and seruynge prestes, so it is also of chantry prestes & brotherhoode prestes in many places. And as it semeth these articles myghte be holpen thus, that is to say, that it be prohibited vpon a payne, that no preeste shall hereafter custumablye vse huntynge, hawkynge, cardes, dyce, nor suche other games vnfyttynge for a preeste, though percase he may as for a recreacion vse some honeste disportes for a tyme: ne custumably vse the ale house or tauerne. And if any preste vse any suche vnlaufull games or other demenour, not conuenient for a preste, so moche that the people be offended by it, and fynde defaut at it, that than if he be warned therof by an abbot and a Justyce of the peace of the shire, where he is dwellynge, and yet he do not reforme hym selfe: that than beside the sayde payne, he be by conuocation suspended fro minystryng the sacramentes, and be dysabled to take any seruice, tyll he be enhabled agayne by the kynge and the ordinarie. And that it be farther enacted, that no man shal haue a chapleyne hereafter, but he haue a stondynge

dynge houſe, and that onely in his ſtondynge houſe, and none to haue a rydyng
chapleyne vnder the degree of a barone,
z that he that hath a ſtondynge houſe /
and hathe alſo a chapleyne / ſhall vppon
a payn prouide for his chapleyn a ſecrete
lodging with locke and key / that he may
lodge fro the commen recourſe of the
laye ſeruantes, and vſe hym ſelfe therin
conueniently in redynge, prayer / or con-
remplatyon, or ſuche other labours and
buſynes as be conuenyente for a preeſte
to vſe.

¶ An other cauſe of the ſayd
dyuyſion.
The ſeuenth Chapyter.

N other occaſyon of the
ſayd dyuyſion hath bene /
by reaſon of dyuers ſutes /
that haue ben taken in the
ſpirituall courtes of office /
that is called in latyn, ex officio : ſo that
the partyes haue not knowen who hath
accuſed them, and thervpon they haue
ſomtyme bene cauſed to abiure in cauſes
of hereſies : ſomtyme to do penaunce, or
to

to pay great sommes of money for rede
myng therof/ which vexation and char-
ges the partis haue thought haue come
to them by the iudges and the offycers
of the spiritualle courte, for they haue
knowen none other accusers, and that
hath caused moche people in dyuers par
tyes of this realme to thynke great malyce and parcialyte in the spirytuall iudges. And if a man be ex officio broughte
before the ordinarye for heresie, if he be
notably suspected of heresye: he muste
pourge him selfe after the wyl of the or-
dinary/ or be accursed, and that is by the
lawe, extra de hereticis . ca. Ad abolen-
dam. And that is thought by many to
be a very harde lawe, for a man may be
suspected and not gyltie/ and so be dryuen to a purgatió without profe or with
out offence in hym, or be accoursed: and
it appereth de hereticis li.vi.in the chapiter In fidei fauorem, rhat they that be
accursed, and also partyes to the same
offence may be wytnes in heresy: and in
the chapiter accusatus pag.licet, it appe
reth/ that if a man be sworne to say the
trouthe concernynge heresie, as well of
L   hym

hym selfe as of other, and he fyrste confesseth nothynge / and after contrary to
his fyrst sayenge he appeleth bothe hym
selfe and other: if it appere by many-
feste tokens, that he dothe it not of light-
nes of mynde, ne of hatred / nor for corruption of money: that than his wytnes in fauoure of the faythe shal stonde /
as well ageynste hym selfe, as agaynste
other: and yet hit appereth euydently
in the same Courte, and in the same
matter, that he is a periured persone.

This is a daungerous lawe, and more
lyke to cause vntrewe and vnlawfulle
men to condempne innocentes, than to
condempne offenders. And it helpethe
lyttell that if there be tokens / that it is
not done of hatred, nor for corruption of
money: that it shulde be taken: for some
time a wolfe may shewe hym selfe in the
apparaile of a lambe. And if the iudge
be parciall, suche tokens may be sooner
accepted than truly shewed. And in the
chapiter there, that begynneth Statuta
quedam / it is decreed, that if the bys-
shoppe or other enquerors of heresy, se
that any great daunger myghte comme
to

to the accusours oz wytnes of herefie by
the great power of them that be accufid:
that than they maye commaunde, that
the names of the accusours oz wytnesse
shal not be shewed but to the byfshop oz
enquerours, oz suche other lerned men
as be called to them, and that shall suffyce, though they be not shewed to the
partie. And foz the moze indempnitie of
the sayde accusours and wytnesse it is
there decreed/that the byfshoppe oz inquerours maye enioyne suche as they
haue shewed the names of suche wytnes vnto, to kepe them close vpon payne
of excōmunication, foz disclosynge that
secrete without theyz lycens. And surely
this is a soze lawe/that a man shall be
condempned, and not knowe the names
of them that be causers therof.
¶ And though the sayd lawe seme to be
made vpon a good consideracion foz the
indempnytie of the accusours and witnes, yet it semeth, that that consydera-
cyon can not suffyce to pzoue the lawe
reasonable. Foz it semeth that the accusours and wytnes myght be saued fro
daunger bi a nother way/and that is by

this way. Jf the bysſhop oʒ inquerours
oʒede, that the accuſours and wytnes
might take hurt, as is ſayd befoʒe : than
might they ſhewe it to the kynge and to
his counſayle , beſechynge his grace of
helpe in that behalſe ⁄ to ſaue and oefend
the accuſours and wytnes fro the extort
power of them that be accuſed : And if
they wold oo ſo : it is not to ſuppoſe ⁄ but
that the kynge wold ſufficiently pʒouide
foʒ theyʒ ſauſe garde : But foʒ as moche
as it ſhulde ſeme , that ſpirituall menne
ſomwhat pʒetende to punyſſhe hereſies
only of theyʒ owne power, without cal-
ling foʒ any aſſiſtance of the tempoʒal po
wer ⁄ therfoʒe they make ſuche lawes, as
may helpe foʒ the theyʒ purpoſe, as they
thynke : but ſurely that is not the charita
ble way ⁄ to put the knowlege of the names of the accuſoʒs and wytnes fro him
that is accuſed, foʒ if he knewe them ⁄ he
might percaſe alledge and pʒoue ſo great
and ſo vehemente cauſe of rancour and
malyce in thé ⁄ that accuſe him, that their
ſayenges by no lawe ought not to ſtonde
agaynſte hym . And that ſpyʒytuall men
pʒetende ⁄ that they only ſhulde haue the
hole

hole inquerie and punyſſhment of hereſi,
it appereth extra de hereticis.li. vi. ca.vt
inquiſitionis, perag. prohibem⁹ : where
all powers/and all lordes temporall and
reulers be prohibite, that they ſhall not
in any maner take knowlege or Judge
vpon hereſie / ſyth it is mere ſpyrytuall,
and he that enquereth of hereſie / taketh
knowlege of heriſie . And ſo the ſumme
called ſumma roſella, taketh it titulo ex-
communicac. perag. iiij . And if that be
true, it ſemeth than, that all iuſtyces of
peace in this realme be excomunicate: for
they by auctoryte of the kynges comiſſy-
ons and alſo by ſtatute, enquere of hereſies. And J thynke it is not in the church
to prohybite that : for though it were ſo,
that the temporall men maye not iudge,
what is hereſie and what not / yet they
may, as it ſemeth, by theyr owne aucto
rytie enquere of it/and enforme the ordy
narie, what they haue founde. And alſo
if a metropolytayne with all his clergye
and people of his dyoces fel into heriſie :
it wolde be herde to redreſſe it without
temporal power. And therfore temporal
men be redye and are bounde to be redy

L 3   to

to oppresse heresies, whan they ryse : as
spiritual men be . And therfore spirituall
men may uot take all the thanke to them
selfe / whan heresyes be punysshed , as
though they charyte and power onely
oyd it, for they haue the fauour and help
of temporalle men to do it, or els many
tymes it wolde not be brought aboute.
Neuertheles myn entent is not to proue
the said lawes al holly to be cruel & vnre
sonable, for J know well / that it is right
expedient, that strayt lawes be made for
punysshment of heresies, that be heresies
in dede, more rather than any other of=
fence, and that the discretion of the iud=
ges spirituell maye ryghte well aswage
the rygour of the sayde lawes / and vse
them more fauorably agaynst them that
be innocent / than agaynst them that be
wylfull offendours , if they wyll chari=
tably serche for the truthe. But surely if
the sayde lawes shulde be putte into the
handelynge of cruell iudges, it myghte
happen that they shuide many tymes pu
nyishe innocentes as wel as offendours,
but J truste in god / it is not so . Neuer
theles whether it be so or not, certaine it

is,

is, that there is a great rumo ur amonge
the people/that it is fo, ꝛ th a t fpirituall
men punyſhe not hereſie onely foꝛ ʒele of
the faith, and of a loue ꝛ a ʒele to the peple with a fatherly pitie to them that fo
offende/as they ought to do/howe great
offenders fo euer they be / but that they
do it rather to oppꝛeſſe them that fpeke
any thynge agaynſt the woꝛldly power
oꝛ rycheſſe of fpyꝛytuall men/oꝛ agaynſt
the great confederacie, that (as many
men faye) is in them to maynteygne it.
And though many fpyꝛytuall men may
be founde, that haue ryght many great
vertues and great gyftes of god as cha-
ſitye / lyberalytye / pacyence, fobꝛenes,
temperaunce, connynge, and fuch other,
yet it wyll be harde to fynde any one
fpyꝛytuall man: that is not enfecte with
the fayd defyꝛe and affection to haue the
woꝛdely honour of pꝛeſtes exalted and
pꝛeferred/ꝛ therfore if any lay má repoꝛt
any euyll of a pꝛeſte/though it be openly
knowen, that it is as he fayth / yet they
wyll be moꝛe dylygent to caufe the laye
man to ceſſe of that fayenge, than to do
that in them is, to refourme that is a

C 4   myſſe

mysse in the preeste / that it is spoken of, takynge as hit were an occasion to doo the lesse in suche reformations, bycause laye men speke so moche ageynst them: But surely that wyll be none excuse to spirituall rulers afore god / whā he shall aske accompte of his people, that were commytted vnto theyr kepynge.

℧ And if this diuision be suffred to continue, it is not vnlyke / but that greate bendynge shall folowe on both parties / wherby greate hurte and inconuenience maye growe vnto moche people. And J see none that may sette a meane way betwene these extremities, ne that mindeth any thynge to do good in it, but the kynges grace and his parlyamente. And J thynke veryly, that they are bounde in conscience to folowe it with effecte, tylle the diuision be clerely cessed. Our lorde of his mercy sende them grace to do it. Amen.

℧ An other occasion of this dyuysion.

The eyght Chapyter.

Jt

T is a commen opinyon a-
mong doctours, that none
is an heretike foz that onely
that he erreth / but foz that
he defendeth opynatyselye
his errour. And therfoze he that erreth
of symplicite may in no wyse be sayd an
heretyke. And summa rosella, in the ty-
tle hereticus in pzincipio, sayeth / that a
man may erre, and meryte therby: and
he putteth this example. If a symple vnlerned man here the pzeachynge of his
byssshop, that pzeacheth happly agaynst
the faithe/and he beleueth it with a redy
mynde to obey: this man meriteth/and
yet he erreth: but that is to be vnderstonde where ignozance excuseth. Than
it semeth, that it is not ynough to pzoue
that a má is an heretike, foz that he hath
holden opinions ayenste that the church
teacheth / ne that he oughte not to make
any purgatyon noz abiuration foz it: foz
that that he hielde in suche case was not
his fayth / but the fayth of the churche
was his fayth, though happly he were
not than fully auysed of it. And therfoze
saynt Aidan, whan he helde the wzonge
L 5 parte

parte of kepynge of Eester, was no heretyke, and some say that saynt Chadde
was of the same opynyon as saynte Ay-
dan was, whiche in lyke wyse was no
heretike/for theyr desyre was to knowe
the truthe: and therfore it is not redde,
that they made eyther purgacyon, or
abiuracion/ne yet the abbotte Joachim,
whiche neuer the lesse erred / for he was
redy to submyt hym to the determyna-
cyon of the church, and therfore he was
neyther holden as an heretyke / ne compelled to abiure. Than if this be sothe,
it were greate pitie if it shulde be true,
as is reported / that there shulde be so
great a desyre in some spyrytuall men to
haue men abiured or haue the extreme
punysshemente for heresie / as it is sayde
there is. For as some haue reported if
any woll wytnes / that a man hath spoken any thynge, that is heresie, though
he speke it onely of an ignoraunce, or of
a passyon, or if he canne by interrogato-
ryes and questyons be dryuen to confesse
any thynge, that is prohybeted by the
churche: a non they wyll dryue hym to
abiure / or holde hym atteynted withoute

oute eramynynge the intente o2 caufe of
his fayenge , o2 whether he hadde a
mynde to be refourmed o2 not : and that
is a verye foo2e waye / oure lo2de be
mo2e mercyfulle to oure foules , than
fo greuoufely to punyffhe vs fo2 eue-
rye lyghte defaute.

And here fome faye, that bycaufe there
is fo.greatte a defy2e in fpy2ytuall men/
to haue men abiure , and to be nooted
with herefie, and that fome / as it were
of a polycye do noyfe hit/ that the royalme is full of heretyckes , mo2e than
it is in dede : that it is verye peryllous,
that fpirituall men fhulde haue auctoritie to arreft a man fo2 euery lyghte fuf-
pection, o2 complaynte of herefye, tylle
that defy2e of punyffhemente in fpirituall men be ceaffed and goone : but that
they fhulde make p2oceffe ageynft them
to b2ynge them in vppon payne of cur-
fynge : and thanne, if they tarye fourty
dayes/the kynges lawes to b2ynge them
in by a w2ytte De excommunicato ca-
piendo / and fo to be b2ought fourthe
out of the kynges Gaole to aunfwere.
But furely, as it is fomewhat touched
befo2e

befoze in the.vii.chap.it femeth that the
church in time paft hath done what they
coulde to bzynge about, that they might
punyffhe herefie of them felfe, without
callynge foz any helpe therin of the fecu-
ler power.

℀And therfoze they haue made lawes
that heretykes myghte be arrefted and
put in pzyfon, and ftokkes yf nede were/
as appereth Clementinis de hereticis .
La.multozum querela. And after at the
fpeciall callynge on of the fpiritualtie, it
was enacted by parlyament , that ozdinaries myght arefte men foz herefie : foz
fomme men thynke, that the fayde Cle-
mentyne was not of effecte in the kynges
lawe to arefte any man foz herefie : But
if a man were openly and notably fufpe-
cted of herefie/and that there were fuffi-
cient recozde and wytnes ayenfte hym,
⁊ there were alfo a doubt that he wold
flee and not appere, wherby he myghte
enfecte other : it femeth conuenient that
he be arefted by the body : but not vpon
euery lyght complaynt, that full lyghtly
maye be vntrewe . And it wyll be right
expedient, that the kynges hyghnes and
                                              his

his counsaylle loke speciallye vpon this
matter / and not to ceaſſe / tylle hit be
bꝛought to moꝛe quietnes than it is yet,
and to ſe with great diligéce, that pꝛide/
couetyſe, noꝛ worldly loue be no iudges/
noꝛ innocentes be punyſſhed/ ne yet that
wylfull offenders go not with out dewe
coꝛreccyon.

℆An other cauſe of this
diuiſion.

The . ix. chapyter.

N other occaſyon of this
dyuyſion hath riſen by the
extremities / that haue ben
ſhewed in ſutes taken in
the ſpirituall courtes / by
ſpirituall menne / foꝛ there
hath therby riſen an opinió among moche people, that a man were as good oꝛ
better to let a ſpyꝛytual man haue at the
begynnyng all that he demaundeth as to
ſtryue with hym in the ſpiritualle lawe
foꝛ it. Jn ſo moche/ that as hit is ſayde/
ſuche extremyties haue bene vſed in the
ſpiri

spirituall lawe for tythes, that no prescription, custome, cóposition, nor other
plee shall be admytted in the spirituall
lawe ageynste them. And surely if that
be trewe, it is a great parcialyte / and a
great denyenge of Justyce. And therfore
it wolde be refourmed. And as for mortuaries they be adnulled all redy by statute, but yet begynnethe to ryse oone
thynge to maynteyne the fyrste diuision
concernynge suche mortuaries, if hit be
suffered to contynue, and that is, that
many curates / not regardynge the kynges statute in that behalfe / perswade
theyr paryshens, whan they be sycke,
to beleue that they can not be saued, but
they restore them as moche as the olde
Mortuarye wolde haue amounted to.
And surelye the Curates / that by that
meanes gette any recompence, by gyfte /
or by queste, are bounde in conscience to
restitution. For he is deceyuedde in his
gyfte or bequeste. For it procedeth not
of a free libertie, but vpon that vntrue
infourmacion. And lyke as a contracte,
wherby a man is deceiued in that thinge
that is solde / holdeth not in conscience,

as if a manne selle copper for golde, or
wyne myrte with water for pure wyne:
and so it is when a man maketh a gyfte
or a bequeste vppon an vntrue surmyse.
And that no man is bounden in conscience to restore for his Mortuary nowe/
sythe the statute of Mortuaryes was
made, it maye appere thus. It is holden by them that be lerned in the lawe
of this royalme, that the parlyamente
hath an absolute power/ as to the pos-
session of all temporall thynges within
this realme, in whose handes so euer
they be/ spyrytualle or temporalle/ to
take them fro oone manne, and gyue
them to an nother, withoute anye
cause or consideration. For if they doo
it, it byndeth in the lawe. And if there
be a consideration, than it byndethe in
lawe and conscience. And certayne
it is, that all suche Mortuaryes were
temporalle goodes, though they were
claymed by spiritualle menne : And
the cause why they were taken awaye
was, for as moche as there were fewe
thynges within this realme, that caused more varyance amonge the people,
than

than they dyd/ whan they were suffred:
for they were taken so farre agaynst the
order of the kynges lawes, and agaynst
Justice and ryght, as shal herafter appere. Fyrste they were taken not onely
after the deth of the husbonde, but also
after the dethe of the wyfe, which after
the lawes of the realme had no goodes/
but that it was taken of the husbondes
goodes/ and they were taken also of seruauntes and chyldren as well infantes
as other. And if a man died by the way,
and had an housholde in an other place,
he shulde paye mortuaries in bothe places. And sometyme whan the parsone/
and vicar of a churche appropried, varied for the mortuaries/ the people, as it
hath ben reported, haue ben entorced/ er
they coulde sytte in reste, to pay in some
places mortuaries to them bothe. And
sometyme the curates wolde prohibyte
poore men to sell theyr goodes in time of
theyr sicknes, if they were suche goodes
as were lyke to be theyr mortuaries: for
they wolde say it was done in defraude
of the church. And if the quyck goodes
were better than the deed goodes/ they
wolde

wolde in some places take the quicke: And yf the deade goodes were better than the quycke, they wolde take the deed. And the Mortuaries muste be delyuered forthe with / or elles the bodye shulde not be buryed. And they prescribed to haue right to Mortuaries onely by the prescription of the spiritual lawe. And vnder that maner mortuaries encreassed dayly in many places , where they hadde not bene vsed before, and of lykelyhode wolde haue gone farther, if they had not bene stopped in tyme. And they were in many places taken in suche maner, that it made the people to think, that the curates loued theyr mortuaries better than theyr lyues. And therypon rose in many places great diuision and grudge betwyxte them , whiche broke the pece, loue, and charite that shulde be betwene the curate and his parysshens , to the great vnquietnes of many of the kynges subiectes / as welle spirituall as temporall / and to the great daunger and perylle of theyr soules . For these causes the said mortuaries be adnulled by parlyament / as well in conscience as in the

D   lawe:

lawe: And yet it is sayd, that some curates vse great extremyties concernynge
the sayde mortuaries, a nother waye:
and that is this. Jf the executours at the
firste requeste pay not the money, that is
appoynted by the statute, they wil anon
haue a citation ayenste hym, And there
he shalbe so handled, that as it is sayde,
it hadde bene mooste commenly moche
better to hym / to haue payde his olde
mortuarie / than the costes and expenses
that he shall paye there. And if it be so /
it wolde de resourmed. And surely this
matter wolde be groundely loked vpon:
for some men saye, that the sute in that
case oughte to be taken in the kynges
courte / and not in the spyrituall courte.

C Other occasions of this
dyuysion.
The tenth Chapyter.

He extreme and couetous
demenour of some curates
with their parishes, wher
of mencion is partly made
hereafter / hath bé an other
cause

cauſe of this diuiſion : And though many ſpirituell men be not felowes with
them i the extremitees : yet none of them
that haue ben beſte and moſt indifferent,
haue not done any thynge to reſourme
them that vſe ſuche extremytees, ne tc
make them thynke/that any defaute is in
them in that doynge : but rather, as it
were with a deffe eare, haue diſſymuled
it,and ſuffered it paſſe ouer/and haue en-
deuozed them ſelfe moze to oppzeſſe all
the lay people, that wolde ſpeke againſt
it / than to reſourme them that do it.
And ſome of the ſayde extremytyes be
thoſe. Some ſay / that in takynge of tythes curates in ſome places wyll haue
the.x.parte of euery thynge within the
paryſſt that is tythable, though theyz
pzedeceſ.ours without tyme of mynde
haue bene contented withoute hit : and
though there be ſufficient beſyde foz the
curate to lyue on/ oz though he hath not
knowen, but that parcas ſome other
thynge in olde tyme hath bene aſſigned
in recompens foz it. And in ſome place is
aſked, as it is ſayde/tythe bothe of che-
kyns and egges / and in ſomme place of

mylke and chefe, and in fome places the
x. parte of the grounde, and alfo of that
that falleth on the grounde. And in fome
places is claymed tithe of feruantes wages without deduction : And it is but in
fewe places/ that any feruaunte fhal go
quyte without fom tyth paying/though
he haue fpent al in fyckenes/ oz vpon his
father and mother, oz fuche other neceffarye expenfes .

And in fom places if a paryfhen haue not
ten calues that yere, the curate wyll put
the tythynge of tyll an other yere, and
than to take a tythe calfe, accomptynge
bothe yeres to gyther, rather than he
wolde the firft yere take the money/that
is in that cafe affygned by the lawe. And
they do lyke wyfe of lambes, pygges,
and fuche other thynges. Alfo in many
places the curates take moze at marya-
ges, buryals, and obytes than they were
wonte to do, and wyll not bury a ftran-
ger/ that dyeth within the paryffhe/but
he haue fome what foz it. Alfo fome curates, whan there is any varyaunce betwene hym and any of his paryfhens, oz
that any of his parifhens be in his dette/
                                    hath

hath prohibyte them from houselle tylle
he be payde. And it hath ben sometyme
sene, that whan a poore man hath bene
sette to be howseled/the curate hath before al the parysshe, vpon some suche dis-
pleasure caused hym to ryse and goo a-
waye/without houselle, to his rebuke.
And though these abusions be not vsed
vniuersallye (god forbede they shulde)
for there be many good curates and o-
ther spirituall men, that wolde not vse
them tor the wynnynge or lesynge of no
erthly thynges : yet whan people of dyuers coûtreys mete to gether, and one of
them telleth an other of some suche extre
mities in some curates in his countreye/
and the other lyke wyse to hym: anone
they esteme suche couetyse and extreme
delynge to be in all curates. And though
they do not well in that doinge, for the
offence of one prieste is no offence to an
other, if they so wyll take it: yet spirituell men do nothynge therin to brynge
the people oute of that iudgement, but
suffre suche abusions to be vsed by some
of thém continually without correction/
and (as J haue sayd before) wyl rather

labour to ſtoppe the mouthes of them,
that wyll fynde defaulte at ſuche deme-
noure , than to helpe to reſourme them/
that do it . And ſurely as longe as they
do ſo/ it wyll be verye harde to haue a
good vnitie τ peas in this behalfe.

℩Other cauſes of the ſayde
dyuyſion.
The .xi. Chapyter.

N nother thynge / that
hath cauſed the people to
grudge agaynſt the poope
and other ſpyrytuall reu-
lers hath bene the graun-
tynge of pardons,foꝛ money. Foꝛ whan
hit hath benne noyſed , that the money
ſhulde be beſtowed to ſomme charitable
vſe, as vppon the buyldynge of ſayncte
Peters churche in Rome, oꝛ to ſuche o-
ther charitable vſe : it hath appered af-
terwarde euidently/that it hath not ben
diſpoſed to that vſe. And that hath cauſed many to thynke, that the ſayde pardons were graunted rather of coueitice/
than of charitie, oꝛ foꝛ the helthe of the
ſoules

foules of the people. And therypon some
haue fallen in maner into dispisynge of
pardons, as though pardons graunted
vppon suche couetise shulde nat auayle.
And becaufe the people be greatly de-
ceyued in that iudgement, for as to the
taker the pardon is good, thoughe the
grantor offende in his grantynge of the
pardon. Therfore it is ryght neceffarye,
that the rulers take hede / that pardons
be hereafter granted in suche charitable
maner / that the people shall haue no occasion ne colour to thynke, that they be
granted of couetice : And than the graū-
tours shall profytte them selfe in theyr
graunte, and the people also in theyr takynge / and elles it maye lyghtely hurte
them bothe . And veryly it were greatte
pitie, that any myslykynge of pardons
shulde growe in the hertes of the people
for any mysdemenour in the grauntours
or other wyfe, for they be right neceffa-
rie. And J suppofe, that if certain pdons
were granted frely without money, for
saying of certeyn prayers therin to be ap
poynted, that all mislykyng of pardons
wolde shortly cesse and vanysshe away

℄An other cause of this
dyuyſion.
The.xij.Chapyter.

Nother cauſe of this di-
uiſion hath ben by reaſon
of dyuers lawes and con-
ſtitutions/which haue ben
made by the church, ſome
tyme by the Pope/ſometyme by lega-
tes/oz by Metropolitanes in theyz pzo-
uince:wherin they haue many tymes ex-
ceded theyz auctozitie, and attempted in
many thynges agaynſte the lawe of the
realme.And yet neuer the leſſe many pzi-
ſtes haue gyuen full credence to them/foz
they haue thought that the makers ther
of, whiche were the heedes of the churche, wolde not make any lawe, but by
good and ſufficient auctozitie. And thervpon it hath folowed/that whan any
doubte oz queſtion hath ryſen vpon the
ſayde lawes : all ſpipitual men in maner
wolde ſticke faſte to the lawes, and many tempozall men by reaſon of a comen
vſe and cuſtome, that they haue ſene to
the contrarie,haue reſiſted them : wher-
vpon

vpon haue rysen in many places greatte
stryse, variaunces, and great expences in
the spirituall lawe. Wherby many temporall men haue thought, that spirytual
courtes be rather vsed for maintenaunce
of couetise/thā for ministracion of iustice.
And thoughe / with the mercye of oure
lorde / the trouthe is not so vniuersally:
yet some diligence wolde be taken to re-
moue that iudgement fro the people.

℃ And of these lawes is the constituti-
on of Boniface the archebysshoppe of
Lanterbury, wherby it is decreed / that
he that letteth a woman couert to make
her wyll, or that letteth it to be proued,
is accursed : and the lawe of the realme
is/that a woman couerte hath no goodes, that she may make any wylle of/ex-
cepte it be of a thynge in action, or that
she were executrix before. And if she were
so, than with lycence of her husbonde
she may make an executour/to the intent
he may leuye the dette/ or fulfyl the firste
wyl. An other lyke lawe is of the decree
of the ryghte reuerende father in god
Robert Wynchelsye, late archbysshoppe
of Lanturbury, made agaynst the comen
D 5   custome

custome of the realme for tithe of wood:
aboue. xx . yere not to be payde / whiche
custome was confermed by the statute
made in the.xlv.yere of kynge E. the.iij.
that is commenly called the statue of
Silua cedua: By reason of whiche decree great sutes, variances, and expenses
haue ensued and wyll ensue/if it be suffered. Wherfore the sayde estatute wolde
be throughly sene : And if it be good,
than not to suffre any decree to stonde
ageynst it / and elles clerely to breake it.
Other lyke lawes be the lawes that be
made by the churche / that executours
shall not / vppon payne of cursynge, ad-
minystre / tyll they haue proued the te-
stament : where the lawe of the realme
is that they may : ¬ so reason wold that
they shulde be : for els the goodes of the
testatour might be embeselled ¬ loste for
euer. And that lay mē may not put clerkes to answer before thē/ specially in cri-
minal causes. And for the strēgth of tho
lawes many spirituall mē haue reported
opély / ¬ that somtime in open sermons/
that such puttyng to answer of pristes be
fore lay men is prohibited by the law of
god,

god,wherypon me thynketh are greatly
to be noted thefe poyntes, that is to fay/
that if it be as they fay, that it is ayenft
the lawe of god, that than great defaut
is in them/ that they haue done no moze
to refourme it than they haue done , foz
cleryng the confciéce of fo many people/
as than daily offend therby. And if it be
not as they fay, than they mainteyne an
vntruth, which is a great offence in men
of fuch grauite τ pfectió/as they be. And
they alfo be therby bouden to reftitution
to the tempozal princis, which ought to
haue theyz fynez τ amerciamentes vpon
fuch futes, as fhuld be taken ageynft priftes in theyz courtes:wherof they be ma
ny tymes excluded by refon of the fayde
pretenfed priuilege. And if it coulde be
fufficiently pzoued/that it is ayenfte the
lawe of god, to put priftes to anfwer be
foze lay men : than degradynge of them
coulde not helpe : Foz not withftanding
the difgradynge,the caracter abydeth/τ
fo he is a prieft ftyll, as he was befoze.
And I fuppofe veryly / that if it coulde
haue ben fufficiétly pzoued/to be ageynft
the lawe of god/the kynges progenitozs
                                    wolde

wolde in tyme paſt haue aſſented to it.
And that the kynges grace and all his
realme, wolde with good wyll alſo con-
foꝛme them ſelf to it/but that was neuer
ſufficiently pꝛoued/as farre as J haue
harde. And to that that ſome ſpirituall
men ſaye, that it is an auncient cuſtome/
and a cuſtome appꝛoued, that pꝛieſtes
in felonies/murthers, and treſons ſhuld
not be putte to auſwere befoꝛe laye men,
and that by reaſon of that olde cuſtome,
they oughte to be pꝛiuileged in that behalfe, though it can not be pꝛoued direct-
ly by the lawe of god: to that it may be
anſwered, that there was neuer yet ſuche cuſtome in this realme apꝛoued. Foꝛ
pꝛieſtes haue ben arayned alway foꝛ treſon and felony befoꝛe the kynges Juſty-
ces. And foꝛ treſon it hath ben ſene, that
they haue ben put in eꝛecution, as it appereth by a compleynt made by the clergye in the parlyament holden in the.xxv.
yere of kynge Edwarde the thyꝛde pꝛo
Clero, where the clergie complayned,
that pꝛieſtes, monkes, ⁊ religious were
contrary to the liberties of the churche
(as they ſayd) put to dethe: and vppon
that

that complaynte it was enacted, that all
maner clerkes, as well secular as religyous, that shulde fro thens fozthe be con-
uicte befoze any Justice secular, foz any
maner of treson oz felony/touching other
persons than the kynge oz his royal ma-
iestie/shulde haue fro thens fozthe freely
the pziuilege of holye churche, and be
without lette oz delaye delyuered to the
ozdinarie, them demaudynge . And it semeth that by that terme, Clerke, in that
statute pzo Clero, is vnderstonde as wel
clercles that be within ozdzes,as clerkes
that can rede as clerkes / and yet be not
within ozdres : foz they shall haue theyz
clergy in petite treson / whiche be commenly taken to be suche treasons, as be
recited in the later ende of the declaracio
of treason, made in the sayde.xxv. yere
of Ed. the.iii. wherof the eschete belon-
geth to the lozdes of the fee . But in the
other treasons,that be recited in the said
Declaration / wherof the fozfayture is
onely to the kynge : none shall haue his
clergy by the common lawe, clerke with
in ozders noz lay man / that can rede / ne
there is not any remedy pzouided foz no
maner

maner of clerkes in tho tresons. For thei
touch the kynge and his royall maiestie.
And therfore they be excepted in the said
statute p̄ Clero, as before appereth, and
be coenly called high treasons : ꝗ of that
nature of treason is nowe wasshing clip
pinge, ꝗ filinge of money : for the statute
made ano.ij.ꞩ.v.is/that it shalbe treson
to the kynge ꝗ to the realme. And therfore no clerke can there haue his clergy.
℃ And here I wolde moue a lytell farther, that if a clerke within ordres bren
a house, bycause he hadde not certayne
money layde in a secrete place, as he appoynted by a byll : whether he shal haue
his pryuylege : for the statute made in
that case, is that suche brennynge shall
be hyghe treason. And yet the forfeiture
is gyuen to the lordes of the fee.ꝛc. And
the sayd statute is anno.viij.ꞩ.vi. ca.vi.
And syth it is haute treason, many men
suppose/that he shall not haue his clergy : but I commytte that to other, that
lyste to treate farther of that matter :
But for counterfaytynge and forgynge
the coyne of an other realme/I suppose
a clerke shulde not be put in execution, if
he

he wyll aske his priuilege. For the statute is no more, but that it shall be treason, and sayeth not that it shall be treason to the kynge and to the realme / as
the other statute dothe. And therfore J
suppose, that by the sayd statute pro clero he shal haue his clergy. yet neuer the
lesse that statute pro clero in one poynte
declareth the common lawe to be more
strayter againste the priuilege of clergy /
than many men take it to be: and that is
in this poynt. Jf a clerke stele any of the
kynges goodes, that he shall not haue
the priuilege of his clergie. For the sayd
statute is, that he shall haue his clergye
in treason or felony concernynge other
persons than the kynge or his royall maiestie. And therfore for felony concerning
the kynge selfe / it semeth that a clerke
at the comen lawe / shulde not haue had
the puilege of his clergie: but that J re-
myt to other, that be lerned in the lawes
of the realme. And J haue spoke the ferther of these matters / because as me semeth, it were ryght expedient / that spirituall men shuld knowe them / & such o-
ther as most specially pteine vnto them,
more

moze parfytely than they haue done in tyme paſt: and moze rather to coueyte to haue the true vnderſtondinge of them, than to repozte/that the makers of them offended in the makynge, ſpecially ſeyng that they were made by the kynge/ with the aſſent of all the lozdes ſpirituall and tempozalle, and of the commens, and ſome of them at the ſpecyall requeſt and peticion of the ſpiritualtie.

℧ And here me thynketh J myght ſaye a lytell farther in is matter / and that (as it is like) the trouth wyl pzoue/ that is to ſay: that as longe as the iuriſdyccions ſpiritual and tempozall be ſuffered to ſtande in ſuche caſe as they do nowe, that tempozall men ſhall ſaye, that ſpirituall men make lawes / that they haue none auctozite to make, and that ſpirytuall men ſhall ſaye, that tempozall men make lawes, that be agaynſt the libertie of the churche, wherfoze they be accurſed, and no other ozder taken to haue it knowen/ what is the libertie of the churche/ and what not/ than is yet taken: Jt wyll be longe er this dyuyſion wyll be fully appeſed . Than to retourne to
the

the priuileges of clerkes . The trouthe
is , that yet clerkes within orders be
more fauoured than clerkes that be not
within ordres. For if a prieste be array-
ned of felony, and confesseth the felony,
or is founde gyltie, and than he prayeth
the benefyte of his priuilege , and sheweth the letters of his ordres: in that
cas the iudges wyll nat compell hym to
rede. For sithe the churche hath admitted hym to orders , the lawe presumeth
that he can rede as many men saye. And
ouer that if a preest wolde wylfully forsake his priuilege, and confesse the felony
and becomme a prouour: yet if the ordinarie wyll aske hym as a membre of
the churche , and shewe the letters of
his orders, he shall haue hym, and that
is by the statute called articuli cleri. For
before that statute he shulde haue bene
compelled to haue done battayle , if the
approuee wolde haue waged hit . And
also if a preeste, after that he hathe con-
fessed the feloni, or after that he is founde
gyltie/ wyll pray his clergie/and after of
wilfulnes he wyll renouce his priuilege:
yet if the ordinarie wyll aske hym, he

E   shall

shall haue hym: and that is by the commen lawe. But in this matter hit is a doubte/ to many men, whether it suffyseth to the ordinary only to affirme, that he is a priest/ι so to aske hym: or that he must shewe the letters of his orders. And I suppose, that it is sufficient, if he affirm that he is within orders, though he shewe not the letters of his orders / nor yet the regestryng of them. And that semeth by the statute of an.iiij. ⅁. vij. ca. xiij. where it appereth, that the Certificat of the ordinarye, that he is within orders, shulde suffyce. And if his certificat shulde suffyce, than it semeth that his scieng in his owne persone, that the other is a clerke, shulde suffyce.

℃ And in the statute made anno. xxiij. Henrici octaui. ca. i. it appereth / that clerkes within holy ordres, haue greatter priuilege, concernynge theyr clergye/ than clerkes, that be not within ordres. But neuer the lesse I leue that matter to the determination of other.

℃ But admitte, that there had ben such accustome receyued and admitted in the realme, that prestes shulde not be put to
aun-

aunſwer befoʒe laye men, and that than
this queſtyon were aſked / whether the
parliament myght bʒeake that cuſtome?
To that queſtyon (as it ſemeth) it maye
be aunſwered thus : That if that cuſtome turne in to an occaſyon and boldeꞏ
nes of theſte and murder, and other lyke
thynges agaynſt the kynges peace, and
that as well in many ſpiʒytuail men as
in tépoʒall men by exáple of ſpiritual mé /
which by reaſon of that pʒiuilege take a
boldnes to offend: Jt were not only a lau
ful dede to bʒeke that cuſtom, but a right
good ⁊ meritoʒious dede to do it and a
dede that the kynge is bounde to at his
coʒonacion. Foʒ he is ſwoʒne to mayn-
teigne the good cuſtomes of his realme,
and to bʒeake the euyll. And ſure it is,
that all cuſtomes / that be agaynſte his
peace, be euyll, as this ſhulde be, if that
effecte ſhulde ſolowe of it, as befoʒe appereth. And that the kynge is ſpeciallye
bounde by his lawes to aduoyde all
thynges / that may be a let to his peace,
it apperyth by the ſtatute that is called
ſtatutú de defentione armoʒú, where it is
ſayd amóge other thynges thus. To the
E 2   kynge

kyng it appertayneth by his royall seignory to defende strongly all armes, and all other force agaynst his peace as ofte as shall please hym. And that he maye punysshe them that do agaynst his peace after the lawes and customes of his realme. And that all his lordes spyrytuall and temporall are bounde to ayde hym therin as theyr souerayne lorde. And syth murders and felonyes are specially agaynst the kynges peace: therfore the sayd custome shulde be agaynst his pece, if suche effecte shulde folowe of it, as before appereth. Wherfore it semeth, that he shuld than haue auctoritie in his parlyamente to breake that custome / as a thynge agaynst the peace and quyetenes of his people. And he that hath auctoritie to aduoyde suche thynges as breke his peace/hath also auctoritie to preuent and deuoyde suche thynges, as maye gyue occasion to the breking of his pece/ as that custome shulde do, if the sayde effecte shulde folowe of it. And certayn hit is, that hit hurteth no more a good prieste, that an euyll preest is punysshed, than it hurteth a lay man/ that he is punysshed:

nyſſhed: ne no moꝛe than it hurteth a
good lay man oꝛ woman, that an other
is euyll and is punyſſhed foꝛ it. And J
ſuppoſe verily, that this diuiſion wyl neuer be perfytely appeaſed, tylle pꝛeeſtes
and religious wyll be as lothe to here of
any defaute in a lay man oꝛ lay woman,
as in a pꝛeſte oꝛ in a relygious perſon.
And that wyll neuer be as longe as the
great confederacies and ſingularite con-
tinueth amonge pꝛeeſtes and amonge religious perſons, as it dothe nowe. The
good lay men and women muſt pacient-
ly beare the euyll repoꝛte of other laye
men and women, that be of the ſame con-
dycyon as they be / and ſo they ſhall be
taught dy ſpiritual men / that they ought
to do : but they wyl not do ſo them ſelfe.
Jn ſo moche that Jſuppoſe verily, that
many a pꝛeſt and religions wold grudge
moꝛe ayenſte an euyll repoꝛte made of a
pꝛeſt oꝛ religious, that in dede were gil-
tie, in pꝛyde / couetiſe, angre / malice, glo-
tony, lecherie, oꝛ ſuche other : than they
wolde be ayenſt a lyke euyl repoꝛt made
of a laye manne oꝛ a laye woman / that
were not gyltie.

⫶Dyuers other lawes there be/that be made by the churche : that many menne thynke the churche hadde no power to make: Zis it is,that no benefice ſhalbe let to a lay man, but a ſpiritual man be ioy‑ ned with hym : Oʒ that it ſhall not be let aboue. iij. yeres. And alſo the conſtitu‑ tion of a dimiſſion noble , ⁊ ſuche other/ that were to longe to reherſe nowe. Foʒ theſe ſuffiſe to ſhew/ that by ſuch lawes made by the churche / that they had no powʒr to make any lawe of/ hath ryſen one ſpeciall cauſe of this diuiſion.

⫶ An other occaſion of this
dyuyſion.
The . xiii. Chapyter.

N other occaſion of this di uiſion hath ryſen by reaſon of feyned viſitations/vſed in tymes paſte by oʒdina‑ ryes and other , that haue hadde power to viſyte houſes of rely‑ gion and churches in the countrey : Foʒ there is a commen opinion in maner vni‑ uerſally ryſen amonge the people , that ſuche

suche visitations/after the maner as they
be vsed do litel good, and rather encrece
vice than vertue. And veryly the moze
pitie is, it semeth to be true as they say.
Foz it is vsed, that at suche visitations,
visitours take of the houses of religion
that they visyte, some certayne pency-
on: And foz visitation of churches they
haue of some certayne church, mete and
dzynke, where they visyte/and than they
gather some certayne duetie of all the
churches within certayn circute in that
contrey. And neuerthe les, as the comen
opinion gothe, comenly they refourme
nothynge/ but as they fynde it/ so they
leue it/ and neyther comfozt they vertue
ne punyshe vice/ but many tymes the
contrarie, by some wozldly demeanour
oz euylle example, that the people see in
them. And thus whan the people haue
sene, that offenders, as well spiritual as
tempozal, contynue after the visitation/
as they dydde befoze: they haue conie-
ctured, that the ozdinaries and visitozs
do visite moze rather foz theyz pencions,
than foz any good ozder oz refozmation.
And this/ thzough a longe continuance/
E 4   hath

hath brought the people to iudge great
couetice in suche visitours / whiche commenly be of the greattest reulers of the
spiritualtie : wherby the people by lyttell and lyttell haue fallen into a dispray-
sing of suche visitations, and into a myslykynge of theyr rulers spiritual / and of
suche pompe and worldly behauour, as
is shewed by them at suche visitations.
And than whan suche visitours and spirituall rulers haue perceyued, that the
people haue misliked theyr visitations,
they haue disdayned it / and haue contynued styll as they dyd before : τ so hath
the grudge betwene them contynued se-
cretely of longe tyme. And surely it is to
be moche meruayled, that visitours wyl
attempte to take at theyr visitations any
pension or imposition of them that they
visite / contrary to the good lawes that
be made in the. vi. boke, ti. de sensibus.
ca. romana, et exigit. Wherin great pe-
nalties be set vppon them that take any
pension at theyr visitations / contrary to
the sayd lawes, as in the same doth appere. And but there be any secret dispensation in that behalfe : many be suspended,

ded/ that dayly ministre. And if there be
any suche secrete dispensation, hit is to
doute/ that the graunte therof proceded
not of charite, but of some couetyse and
singularite: yf the very grounde therof
were throughly serched. Wherfore hit
were ryght expedient, that suche visita‧
tions were set in suche order/ as well by
spirituall authorite/ as by temporal auc‧
torite/ that good men hereafter myght
therby be comforted, and euyll men cor‧
rected & reformed / to the good example
of all other that shulde here of it.

⸿An other cause of this
diuision.
The. xiiij. Chapyter.

A not her cause of the said
diuision hath rysen by oc‧
casion of the great multi‧
tude of lycences and dispen
sations, that haue benne
made for money by popes and busshops
in tyme paste, contrary to dyuers good
lawes made by the churche, as of plu‧
ralites, ayenst the lawe that no mā shuld

haue but one benefice / and of lycence to curates to be none reſident, of capacities to men of relygyon / and that none ſhall take orders, ne be promoted afore a certayne age, and ſuche other: whiche lycences and diſpenſacions haue bene ſo accuſtomably graunted for money without cauſe reaſonable, that great inconuenyences haue folowed vppon it, to the great grudge, and murmour, and euyll example to all the people.

An other cauſe of the ſayde dyuyſion. The.xv. Chapyter.

AN other occaſyon of the ſayd diuiſion hath ryſen by a great laxnes and lyberty of lyuynge / that the people haue ſene in many religious men. For they ſay / that though religious men profeſſe obedience and pouerty / yet many of them haue ⁊ wil haue their owne wil / with plenty ⁊ delicate fedynge / in ſuche abundance that no obedience nor pouertie appereth in them.

And

And therfore many haue sayde, and yet
say to this day/ that religious men haue
the most pleasant & delicate lyfe that any
men haue. And truly if we behold the ho
lynes & blessed examples of holy fathers,
& of many relygyous persons / that haue
bene in tyme past and of many religious
persons that be now in these dayes: we
shulde se ryght great diuersity bytwene
them, I trowe (as for many of them)as
great diuersitie as is bytwene heuen and
hell. And here, as it semeth, I myght
conueniently reherse the wordes that be
spoken in the fyrst boke of the folowynge
of Chryste, the xviij.chapyter/where it
speaketh of the holy fathers, that haue
bene in religion in tyme past, and sayeth
thus. They serued our lorde, in hunger
and in thurste, in hete and in colde, in na
kednes, in labour, and in werynes, in vi-
gils and fastinges/ in prayers, and in holye meditations, in persecucions / and in
many reproffes. They refused honours
here in this lyfe, that they myght alway
haue them in the euerlasting life. O how
strayt and howe abiecte a lyfe led the ho
ly fathers in wyldernes? howe greuous
tempta-

temptacions they suffered: howe fyersly
they were with theyr ghostly enemyes
assailed? howe feruent prayer they dayly offered to god? what rygorous absti-
nence they vsed? howe great zele and fer
uour they had to spirituall profite? how
stronge bataylle agaynst all synne? And
howe pure and holle entent they hadde
to god in al theyr dedes? on the day they
laboured/ and on the night they prayed.
And though they laboured on the daye
bodily/yet they prayed in mynde, and so
they spente theyr tyme alway frutefully/
and thought euery houre shorte: for the
seruyce of god, and for the great swete-
nes that they hadde in heuenly contemplation, they forgette ofte tymes theyr
bodily refection. All ryches, honour, di-
gnities, kinnesmen, and frendes they renounced for the loue of god. They coue-
ted to haue nothynge of the worlde, so
that scarcely they wolde take that was
necessarye for the bodilye kynde. They
were poore in worldly goodes/but they
were ryche in grace and vertues. They
were nedy outwardely, but inwardely
they were replenysshed with grace and
ghostly

goostly comfortes. To the worlde they were alyens and straungers, but to god they were ryghte deere and famylyer frédes. In the syghte of the worlde and in theyr owne sighte they were vile and abiecte / but in the sight of god & of his saynctes they were precious and singularly electe. In them shone all perfection of vertu, trewe mekenes / symple obedience, charite, and pacience, with other like vertues and gracious giftes of god. Wherfore they profited dayly in spirite/ and opteyned great grace of god. They be lefte as an exaumple to all religious persones, and more oughte theyr examples to stere them to deuocion, and to profite more & more in vertue and grace/ than the great multitude of dissolute and ydle persones shulde any thynge drawe them abacke . O what feruoure was in religious persons at the begynnynge of theyr religion ? What deuocion in prayers, what zele to vertue / what loue to goostly discipline / and what reuerence and meke obedience flourisshed in them vnder the rule of theyr superiour ? truely theyr dedes yet bere witnes, that they

were

were holy and perfyte, that so myghtly
subdued the worlde, and thrust it vnder
fote. Thus farre gothe the sayde chap-
ter. But the more pitie is, most men say,
that nowe a dayes many religious men
wyl rather folow theyr owne wyl, than
the wylle of theyr superiour, and that
they wyll neyther haue hunger nother
thyrst/ heate/ nor colde: nakednes, wery-
nes/ nor labour/ but riches honor/ digni-
ties fredes & worldly acqueintace, atté-
dance of seruátes at their comandemen-
tes, plesures, disportes & that more libe-
rally than temporall mé haue. Thus are
they fallé (say they) fro the true religió:
wherby the deuocion of the people is in
maner fallé fro thé. Neuertheles J dout
not/ but there be many right good & ver
tuous religious persones/ god forbide it
shulde be otherwyse : but hit is sayde/
that there be many euyll, and that in su-
the multitude, that they that be good
canne not, or wyll not, see them resourmed. And one great cause that lettethe
resourmation in this behalse / is this:
Jf the moste dissolute persone in all the
cóminaltie/ and that lyueth moste openly
ayenst

ayenſt the rules of the religion, can vſe
this policye, to extolle his religion a-
boue other, and diſpꝛayſe other rely-
gyons / foꝛ that they be not of ſuche
perfeccyon as theyꝛ relygion is, anoue
he ſhall be called a good ſeruente bꝛo-
ther, and oone that beareth vppe the
religion, and ſhall be therfoꝛe the moꝛe
lyghtely foꝛboꝛne in his offences.

Where the trouthe is, that the religion
maynteyneth hym, and bearethe vppe
hym / and not he the religion. Foꝛ hit
hath lyttell nede of hym. And though
many be good / and lyue a ryght good
and laudable lyfe, after the ſtatutes and
oꝛder there vſed : yet in that poynt / to
extolle their religyon aboue other, and
to take parte with them, that doo ſo,
though they knowe, that they that ſo
extoll it, kepe not the religion them ſelfe /
ſewe be without offence / and truly that
is a great defaute / foꝛ it gyueth a great
boldnes to offenders, and diſcourageth
them, that be good, whanne they ſee
them that moſte lyue ayenſte theyꝛ relygion / be ſo maynteygned and commen-
ded.

An

¶An other thing that hath caused many people to myslike religion, hath ben the great extremite/that hath ben many tymes sene at elections of abbottes, priours, and suche other souerayngnes spirituall. And this is a gencrall grounde, that whan religious men perceyue, that the people myslike them, they in theyr hartes withdrawe their fauour and deuocion agayne fro them: And so hath charitie waxed colde betwene them.

And veryly J suppose / that hit were better, that there shulde no abbotte or pryoure hereafter contynue ouer certayne yeres, that shuld be appoynted by auctorite of the rulers, than to haue suche extremites at elections, as haue ben vsed in tyme past in many places.

¶And verely (as me semeth) one thing wolde do great good concernynge relygions, and all relygious persons, and that is this: that the rules and constitutions of religion were sene and wel considered, whether the rygour and straytnes of them may be borne nowe in these dayes/ as they were at the beginnyng of the religions. For the people be nowe

moze weyke / as to the multitude / than
they were than. And if it be thought /
that they may not be nowe kepte: that
than suche relaxacions and interpzetati-
ons of theyz rules be made, as shall be
thought by the reulers expedient: Foz
bettre it is to haue an esye rule wel kept,
than a strayte rule bzoken without coz-
rection: Foz therof foloweth a boldnes
to offende, a quyet herte in a euyl conscy-
ence: a custome in synne, with many e-
uyll examples vnto the people: wherby
many haue founde defaut at all religion,
where they shulde rather haue founde
defaute at dyuers abusions agaynst the
true religion: Foz certayne it is / that religions were first made by holy fathers,
by the instincte of the holy ghoste / kepe
them who so may.

℧The conclusyon of this lyttell treatice.

The. xvi. Chapiter.

F   Sith

Ythe there is no sacrifyce that more pleseth almyghty god/ than zele of soules dothe/it is good that euery man dispose hym selfe, as nygh as he can/ to haue that zele: And if he may through grace come thervnto,it shall instructe hym in many thynges, how he shal behaue him selfe anenste his neyghbour. And fyrste hit shall teache hym/ that he shall take hede,that he do nothynge/that myght gyue occasion vnto his neyghbour to offende. And J vnderstonde not therby, that he shall only take hede, that he do none euyll dede, wherby his neyghboure maye take occasion to offende, whiche in latyn is called offendiculum/ that is to say/ an occasion to offende : but J meane also, that he shall take hede/ that his neyghboure take none occasion to offende by no dede that he shall do, though it be good, as gyuinge of almes, or buyldynge of churches, or such other : which if the people iuged to be done of pryde τ vaine glory/ must be lefte for a tyme, for hurtynge of them that be of that opynion/ tyll they

may

maye be inſtructed of the intente of the
dede. And if they wyll in no wyſe be refourmed, than bycauſe hit ſemeth to be
of malice, as was in the phariſeys: their
iudgement may be diſpyſed/ᵹ the good
dede contynued.

℧ Alſo where trouth ſhulde peryſſhe/if
the good dede ſhulde be omytted / there
a good dede is not to be omytted . And
accordynge to that is ſayde before/ the
bleſſed apoſtell ſaynt Paule, of a greatte
ʒele that he had to the people / ſayde :

℧ If eatynge of fleſſhe ſhulde hurte my
neyghbour, J wolde neuer eate fleſſhe.
And therfore in the ſayd chapiter he mo-
nyſſhed all them, that wolde eate mete,
that was offered to ydolles before them
that were newly conuerted of the gen-
tyles/and that were yet but weke in the
faythe : that they ſhulde beware , that
though they knewe, that they myghte
laufully do as they dydde, that yet they
ſhulde take hede , that theyr brother
were not offended therby. And in al that
chapiter the holy apoſtell treateth moch
that it is good to euery man to be ware/
that through his dede he gyue no occa-

ſion

sion to his brother to offende. And J beseche almyghty god, that euery manne/
but moost specially our lordes and may-
sters spyrytuall/ may hereafter endeuor
them selfe to kepe wel this poynt/that is
to say/ that they do nothyng to gyue the
people occasyon to offende : and ouer
that, that they may diligently instructe
the vnlerned people to the knowlege of
the trouthe, and to stable them as well
by doctrine as by good example, all singularite sette aparte . And for as moche
as doctrine and good example perteyne
moste specially to prelates and spirituall
rulers, therfore J shall brefely recyte certayne auctorities, that shall some what
moue them to haue a zele and loue vnto
the people. And also to be pyteous vnto
them : And for shortenes J shall omytte
for this tyme to shewe by whome the
sayd auctorities were spoken/besechyng
the reders to take hede to the wordes
that be spoken, though hit appere not
who speake them.

℃ Fyrst J fynde dyuers auctorities that
say thus : Jt is expedient, that prelates
study more to profite the people, than to
                                                    haue

haue preeminence ouer the people.

℄ Also J fynde wrytten / that thoughe punisſhment may not holly be omytted / that yet it profyteth moche, that hit be sometyme deferred.

℄ Also that it behoucth neceſſarily, that he that hath rule ouer other / bréne euer in a quycke lyuely zele to the helthe of they: soules, that he hath rule of : And that els he ſhal lytell profyte vntothem. And therfore he couceth vndiscretely to haue rule ouer them / that he studyethe not to profite vnto. And therfore this is sayde ſpecially to prelates and to other that haue rule ouer the people : Rule ye, to foresee the perylles and daungers of them that ye haue rule of, to counfaylle them to procure their helth, and to ſerue and to profite to other / as good faythfull and wyſe seruauntes, whome our lorde hath ordeyned ouer his houſeholde.

Plante ye vertue in them by holſomme doctryne, water it by good example, and helpe them with your prayour, and thã haue ye done that perteineth to you / and our lorde ſhall well gyue encrece of growynge, whan hit ſhall pleaſe hym, and

that parauenture there as after mannes
iugement was farre vnlyke. These thre
thynges therfore be very necessary, doctryne, example / and prayour, but the
greattest of them is prayour. It is also sayd to the prelates thus : Knowe ye,
that ye oughte to be as mothers to the
people , and not as lordes / and ye
ought to studye rather to be beloued thā
dred, and if it be necessary some tyme to
haue correction, that it be a fatherly correction, and not as it were of a tyraunte/
and show your selfe as mothers in noris-
shynge of the people / and as fathers in
correctyng them. Be meke/put away all
fiersenes/forbere beting/ᇎ speke vnto the
people faire ᇎ sobre wordes, and set not
your yock to greuously vpon thē, whose
burdeyns ye ought rather to bere. If ye
be spiritual, instruct the people in the spi-
rite of Softenes, ᇎ let euery man cōsidre
hym selfe well, leest that he may be also
tempted . De that is a mother dyssy-
muleth not/ he can ioye with them that
ioye/wepe with them that wepe/and he
wylle not ceasse to thruste oute of the
breste of compassion the mylke of consola
tion.

tion. He taketh hede, if he can perceyue
any mã/that is vered with any gret tép-
tacion oz trouble /ꞇ that is heuy ꞇ weike
therwith: And if he finde any such, with
him he sozoweth, him louingly he entre-
teth him he cófozteth,ꞇ findeth anon mã
ny argumétes of pitie ꞇ trust, wherwith
he reiseth him vp ayen to cófozt of spirit.
And if he knowe any that is pzompte/
quick,ꞇ wel pzofityng in grace/he ioyeth
with hym,he giueth him many holsome
counsailes, ꞇ kindeleth him/and instruc-
teth hym all that he can to perceuer and
pzofyte euer fro better to better, he con-
fozmeth him selfe to euery mã,he tozneth
the affections of al men vnto hym selfe in
al goodnes,and pzoueth him selfe verily
to be a mother, as well of them that be
offenders,as of them that pzofiteth in
grace : And as a trewe leche he se-
keth as well them that be sycke as them
that be hoole / and all this he dothe
thzough the gifte of pitie, and of a zele,
that he hath to the helth of theyz soules.
Also a good diligente shepeherde neuer
cessethe to fede his flocke with good les-
sons and exaumples, and that with his

owne example rather than with other
mennes. For if he fede them with other
mens examples/and not with his owne/
hit is but a rebuke vnto hym , and his
flocke shall not profyte moche therby.

For if a prelate wyl shewe vnto the people the sobrenes of Moyses/the pacience
of Job, the mercy of Samuell, the ho-
lynes of Dauyd, & suche other examples
of blessed men: and he hym selfe be vn-
meke, vnpacient, vnmercyfulle, and not
holy/ it is to fere/ that al those examples
shal lytel profite. And therfore prelates,
that in tyme passed haue bene the verye
trewe shepeherdes, though they hadde
theyr bodyes here of the erth/yet neuer
the lesse they fed the flockes of our lorde
to them commytted with heuenly sode,
and vsed not to preache to them theyr
owne wylle, but the wylle of god. And
one man saythe of prelates this : whan
J (sayth he) beholde the heyght of the
honour of prelacy, forthe with J drede
the peryll and daunger of it. And whan
J considre the degree, J drede the ruine.
J consydre the heyghte of the dignitie,
and J beholde forthwith the mouthe of
Delle

Welle open euen at hande. For there is
no doubt, but that theyr administration
is more peryllous, than is the minystra-
tion of any other. But yet neuerthelesse
if they administre wel/they shal get them
selfe therby an hyghe degree in heuen/ꝗ
they shall receiue the gretter abundance
and more full measure of peace for theyr
good trauaylle for euer. And I beseche
almyghty god to sende these. iiii. thynges habundantly into the worlde / and
that mooste specially amonge prelates,
and spirituall rulers/ that is to say , ȝele
of soules, pitie, good doctryne, and de-
uout prayour. And than vndoubtedly,
a newe lyghte of grace, and of tractabi-
litie, shall shortely shewe and shyne a-
moge the people.

⸿ Thus endeth this Treatyse
concernynge the diuision
betwene the spiri-
tualtie ꝗ the
tem-
poraltie .
⸿

TABVLA·

yrste that the dyuysyon a-
mong spyrytual men them
selfe hath bene one cause of
the dyuysion/ that is nowe
bytwene the spyrytualtye
and temporalty in this realme.

The firste Chapiter.

℃ That the omittynge of dyuers good
lawes/with certaine defautes and disor-
der in men of the church/whiche among
other be recited and declared by Jhoñ
Gerson: haue bene an other occasion of
this dyuysion.

The seconde Chapiter.

℃ That certayne lawes made by the
churche, wherin it is recited, quod laici
sunt clericis infesti, that is to saye, that
laye men be cruell to clerkes: hath bene
an other cause of this dyuysion.

The thyrde Chapiter.

℃ That the extreme lawes made by the
church for leyenge violent handes vpon
clerkes / haue bene an other cause of this
dyuysion.   The fourth Chapiter.

That

¶That the disorderynge of the generall sentence hath bene an nother occasyon of the sayde diuision.

The fyfte Chapyter.

¶That an other occasion of this diuysion hath partly rysen by temporal men, through disordrynge of theyr chapleyns and chauntrye preestes.

The syxte Chapiter.

¶That sutes taken in the spiritual courtes (ex officio) haue ben an nother occasyon of this diuision.

The seuenth Chapyter.

¶That though after the determination of doctours/ a man is not an heretyke, for that only that he erreth, but for that he opinatyfely defendeth his errour, and that neuer the lesse the spiritualtie, as a commen voyce gothe amonge the people, haue in tyme paste punysshed many for heresie vpon lyght causes and offences, wherypon many people haue grudged/ and that grudge hath ben an other occasyon of this diuysion.

The eyght Chapiter.

¶That the parcialite that hathe benne shewed vpon sutes taken in the spiritual courte court by spiritual mē, hath ben an other cause of this diuision.

The nynthe Chapyter.

¶ That the extreme and couetous demenour of some curates with theyr parysshens, hath ben an other cause of this diuision.   The tenth Chapiter.

¶ That the grauntynge of pardons for money, as it were to some charytable vse, that hath not after folowed, hathe raised an other grudge amonge the people, whiche hath ben an other occasion of this diuision.

The leuenth Chapiter.

¶ That the makynge of lawes by the church, whiche they had none auctorite to make, hath ben an other occasion of this diuisyon.

The twelthe Chapitre.

¶ That lacke of good visitations hath ben an other occasion of this diuision.

The thyrtene chapiter.

¶ That the great multitude of lycences and dispensacions made by spirytuall rulers for money vpon lyghte suggestions hath ben an other cause of this diuision.

The fouretene.   Chapiter.

That

THE TABLE.

℄ That the great laxnes and worldely pleasures of religious persons / wherby the people hath benne greatly offended, hath bene an other occasion of this diuysion. **The fystene Chapiter.**

℄ Than for a conclusion of this treatise it is som what touched, howe good it is to haue a zele of soules, and how perillous it is to do any thynge, wherby they myght be hurted. And that if zele of soules/pitie/good doctrine, ꝗ deuoute prayour, were abundauntly in this worlde / moost specially in prelates and spirituall rulers : that than a newe lyght of grace and tractabilite, wolde shortelye shewe and shyne amonge the people.
The. xvi. Chapiter.

℘ Londini in edibus Thome Bertheleti, prope aquagium sitis
sub intersignio Lucre
cie Romane
excus.

CVM PRIVILEGIO.